My Anti-Inflammatory Diet

A Different Cookbook for Your Anti-Inflammatory Diet

Camila Allen

Disclaimer Notice:

Table of Contents

Salmon and Lime Potatoes

Prep Time: 10 min | **Cook Time:** 25 min | **Serve:** 4

- 4 salmon fillets, boneless

- 1 garlic cloves, minced

- 2 tablespoons olive oil

- A pinch of salt and black pepper

- 1 yellow onion, sliced

- 2 sweet potatoes, peeled and cut into wedges

- 1 tablespoon rosemary, chopped

- 1 tablespoon lime juice

1.Grease a baking dish with the oil, arrange the salmon, garlic, onion and the other ingredients into the dish and bake everything at 380 degrees F for 25 minutes.

2.Divide the mix between plates and serve.

Nutrition: calories 260, fat 4, fiber 6, carbs 10, protein 16

Salmon with Coconut Sauce

Prep Time: 5 min | **Cook Time:** 20 min | **Serve:** 4

- 3 tablespoons olive oil

- 4 salmon fillets, boneless

- 4 garlic cloves, minced

- ¼ cup coconut cream

- 1 tablespoon parsley, chopped

- 1 tablespoon rosemary, chopped

- 1 tablespoon basil, chopped

- 1 tablespoon oregano, chopped

- 1 tablespoon pine nuts, toasted

- A pinch of salt and black pepper

1.In a blender, combine the oil with the garlic and the other ingredients except the fish and pulse.

2.Arrange the fish in a roasting pan, add the herbed sauce on top and cook at 380 degrees F for 20 minutes.

3.Divide the mix between plates and serve.

Nutrition: calories 386, fat 26.8, fiber 1.4, carbs 3.5, protein 35.6

Turmeric Shrimp Mix

Prep Time: 5 min | **Cook Time:** 12 min | **Serve:** 4

- 1 pound shrimp, peeled and deveined

- 2 tablespoons olive oil

- 1 teaspoon cumin, ground

- 4 green onions, chopped

- 1 cup canned black beans, drained and rinsed

- 2 tablespoons lime juice

- 1 teaspoon turmeric powder

1.Heat a pan with the oil over medium heat, add the green onions and sauté for 2 minutes.

2.Add the shrimp and the other ingredients, toss, cook over medium heat for another 10 minutes, divide between plates and serve.

Nutrition: calories 251, fat 12, fiber 2, carbs 13, protein 16

Shrimp and Lime Spinach

Prep Time: 10 min | **Cook Time:** 10 min | **Serve:** 4

- 1 pound shrimp, peeled and deveined
- 2 tablespoons olive oil
- 1 tablespoon lime juice
- 1 cup baby spinach
- A pinch of sea salt and black pepper
- 1 tablespoon chives, chopped

1.Heat the pan with the oil over medium heat, add the shrimp and sauté for 5 minutes.

2.Add the spinach and the remaining ingredients, toss, cook the mix for another 5 minutes, divide between plates and serve.

Nutrition: calories 206, fat 6, fiber 4, carbs 7, protein 17

Lime Cod Mix

Prep Time: 10 min | **Cook Time:** 15 min | **Serve:** 4

- 4 cod fillets, boneless

- 2 tablespoons olive oil

- 4 spring onions, chopped

- Juice of 1 lime

- 1 red bell pepper, cut into strips

- 1 green bell pepper, cut into strips

- 2 teaspoons parsley, chopped

- A pinch of salt and black pepper

1.Heat a pan with the oil over medium heat, add the bell peppers and the onions and sauté for 5 minutes.

2.Add the fish and the rest of the ingredients, cook the mix for 10 minutes more, flipping the fish halfway.

3.Divide the mix between plates and serve.

Nutrition: calories 180, fat 5, fiber 1, carbs 7, protein 11

Cod and Tomato Pan

Prep Time: 5 min | **Cook Time:** 20 min | **Serve:** 4

- 1 pound cod fillets, boneless and cubed
- 2 tablespoons avocado oil
- 1 avocado, peeled, pitted and cubed
- 1 tomato, cubed
- 1 tablespoon lemon juice
- ¼ cup parsley, chopped
- 1 tablespoon tomato paste
- ½ cup veggie stock
- A pinch of sea salt and black pepper

1.Heat a pan with the oil over medium-high heat, add the fish and cook for 3 minutes on each side.

2.Add the rest of the ingredients, cook the mix for 14 minutes more over medium heat, divide between plates and serve.

Nutrition: calories 160, fat 2, fiber 2, carbs 4, protein 7

Shrimp and Balsamic Zucchinis

Prep Time: 5 min | **Cook Time:** 8 min | **Serve:** 4

- 1 pound shrimp, peeled and deveined

- 2 tablespoons avocado oil

- 2 zucchinis, sliced

- Juice of 1 lime

- A pinch of salt and black pepper

- 2 red chilies, chopped

- 3 garlic cloves, minced

- 1 tablespoon balsamic vinegar

1.Heat a pan with the oil over medium-high heat, add the shrimp, garlic and the chilies and cook for 3 minutes.

2.Add the rest of the ingredients, toss, cook everything for 5 minutes more, divide between plates and serve.

Nutrition: calories 211, fat 5, fiber 2, carbs 11, protein 15

Rosemary Scallops

Prep Time: 10 min | **Cook Time:** 10 min | **Serve:** 4

- 2 tablespoons olive oil

- 1 pound sea scallops

- ½ teaspoon rosemary, dried

- ½ cup veggie stock

- 2 garlic cloves, minced

- Juice of ½ lemon

1.Heat a pan with the oil over medium-high heat, add the garlic, the scallops and the other ingredients, cook everything for 10 minutes, divide into bowls and serve.

Nutrition: calories 170, fat 5, fiber 2, carbs 8, protein 10

Crab and Tomato Salad

Prep Time: 5 min | **Cook Time:** 0 min | **Serve:** 4

- 1 cup canned crab meat, drained
- 1 pound shrimp, peeled, deveined and cooked
- 1 cup cherry tomatoes, halved
- 1 cucumber, sliced
- 2 cups baby arugula
- 2 tablespoons avocado oil
- 1 tablespoon chives, chopped
- 1 tablespoon lemon juice
- A pinch of salt and black pepper

1.In a bowl, combine the shrimp with the crab meat and the other ingredients, toss and serve.

Nutrition: calories 203, fat 12, fiber 6, carbs 12, protein 9

Garlic Salmon with Zucchinis

Prep Time: 10 min | **Cook Time:** 30 min | **Serve:** 4

- 4 salmon fillets, boneless
- 2 tablespoons avocado oil
- 2 tablespoons sweet paprika
- 2 zucchinis, sliced
- 2 tomatoes, cut into wedges
- ¼ teaspoon red pepper flakes, crushed
- A pinch of sea salt and black pepper
- 4 garlic cloves, minced

1.In a roasting pan, combine the salmon with the oil and the other ingredients, toss gently and cook at 370 degrees F for 30 minutes.

2.Divide everything between plates and serve.

Nutrition: calories 210, fat 2, fiber 4, carbs 13, protein 10

Shrimp and Spinach Salad

Prep Time: 5 min | **Cook Time:** 0 min | **Serve:** 4

- 1 pound shrimp, cooked, peeled and deveined
- 2 mangoes, peeled and cubed
- 3 scallions, chopped
- 1 cup baby spinach
- 1 cup baby arugula
- 1 jalapeno, chopped
- 2 tablespoons olive oil
- 1 tablespoon lime juice
- A pinch of salt and black pepper

1.In a bowl, combine the shrimp with the mango, scallions and the other ingredients, toss and serve.

Nutrition: calories 210, fat 2, fiber 3, carbs 13, protein 8

Coconut Cod

Prep Time: 5 min | **Cook Time:** 20 min | **Serve:** 4

- 2 tablespoons olive oil

- 1 pound cod fillets, boneless and cubed

- 2 spring onions, chopped

- 2 garlic cloves, minced

- 1 cup coconut cream

- ¼ cup chives, chopped

- A pinch of salt and black pepper

- 2 tablespoons Dijon mustard

1.Heat a pan with the oil over medium heat, add the garlic and the onions and sauté for 5 minutes.

2.Add the fish and the other ingredients, toss, cook over medium heat for 15 minutes more, divide into bowls.

Nutrition: calories 211, fat 5, fiber 5, carbs 6, protein 15

Trout and Lemon Sauce

Prep Time: 5 min | **Cook Time:** 15 min | **Serve:** 4

- 4 trout fillets, boneless

- 2 tablespoons avocado oil

- 1 cup cilantro, chopped

- 2 tablespoons lemon juice

- ½ cup coconut cream

- 1 tablespoon walnuts, chopped

- A pinch of salt and black pepper

- 3 teaspoons lemon zest, grated

1.In a blender, combine the cilantro with the cream and the other ingredients except the fish and the oil and pulse well.

2.Heat a pan with the oil over medium heat, add the fish and cook for 4 minutes on each side.

3.Add the cilantro sauce, toss gently and cook over medium heat for 7 minutes more.

4.Divide the mix between plates and serve.

Nutrition: calories 212, fat 14.6, fiber 1.3, carbs 2.9, protein 18

Cilantro Tilapia

Prep Time: 5 min | **Cook Time:** 12 min | **Serve:** 4

- 4 tilapia fillets, boneless

- 2 tablespoons olive oil

- 2 tablespoons lemon juice

- 1 teaspoon basil, dried

- 1 tablespoon cilantro, chopped

1.Heat a pan with the oil over medium heat, add the fish and cook for 5 minutes on each side.

2.Add the rest of the ingredients, toss gently, cook for 2 minutes more, divide between plates and serve.

Nutrition: calories 201, fat 8.6, fiber 0, carbs 0.2, protein 31.6

Salmon and Mustard Sauce

Prep Time: 5 min | **Cook Time:** 14 min | **Serve:** 4

- 4 salmon fillets, boneless
- ½ teaspoon mustard seeds
- ½ cup mustard
- 2 tablespoons olive oil
- 4 scallions, chopped
- Salt and black pepper to the taste
- 2 green chilies, chopped
- ¼ teaspoon cumin, ground
- ¼ cup parsley, chopped

1.Heat a pot with the oil over medium heat, add the scallions and the chilies and cook for 2 minutes.

2.Add the fish and cook for 4 minutes on each side.

3.Add the remaining ingredients, toss, cook everything for 4 more minutes, divide between plates and serve.

Nutrition: calories 397, fat 23.9, fiber 3.5, carbs 8,5, protein 40

Shrimp and Turmeric Cauliflower

Prep Time: 10 min | **Cook Time:** 10 min | **Serve:** 4

- 2 tablespoons olive oil
- 1 pound shrimp, peeled and deveined
- 1 cup cauliflower florets
- 2 tablespoons lemon juice
- 2 tablespoons garlic, minced
- 1 teaspoon cumin, ground
- 1 teaspoon turmeric powder
- Salt and black pepper to the taste

1.Heat a pan with the oil over medium-high heat, add the garlic and sauté for 2 minutes.

2.Add the shrimp and cook for 4 minutes more.

3.Add the remaining ingredients, toss, cook the mix for 4 minutes, divide between plates and serve.

Nutrition: calories 200, fat 5.3, fiber 3, carbs 11, protein 6

Salmon and Cilantro Broccoli

Prep Time: 5 min | **Cook Time:** 15 min | **Serve:** 4

- 4 salmon fillets, boneless

- 1 teaspoon coriander, ground

- 1 cup broccoli florets

- 2 tablespoons lemon juice

- 2 tablespoons avocado oil

- 1 tablespoon lemon zest, grated

- A pinch of salt and black pepper

- 2 tablespoons cilantro, chopped

1.Heat a pan with the oil over medium heat, add the fish and cook for 4 minutes on each side.

2.Add the broccoli and the other ingredients, cook the mix for 7 more minutes, divide between plates and serve.

Nutrition: calories 210, fat 4.7, fiber 2, carbs 11, protein 17

Nutmeg Salmon and Mushrooms

Prep Time: 10 min | **Cook Time:** 20 min | **Serve:** 4

- 4 salmon fillets, boneless

- 2 tablespoons olive oil

- 1 cup mushrooms, sliced

- 3 green onions, chopped

- 1 tablespoon lime juice

- ¼ teaspoon nutmeg, ground

- ¼ cup almonds, toasted and chopped

- A pinch of salt and black pepper

1.Heat a pan with the oil over medium-high heat, add the green onions and sauté for 5 minutes.

2.Add the mushrooms and cook for 5 minutes more.

3.Add the fish and the other ingredients, cook it for 5 minutes on each side, divide between plates and serve.

Nutrition: calories 250, fat 10, fiber 3.3, carbs 7, protein 20

Chili Shrimp with Scallions Rice

Prep Time: 10 min | **Cook Time:** 25 min | **Serve:** 4

- 1 pound shrimp, peeled and deveined
- 1 cup black rice
- 2 cups chicken stock
- 4 scallions, chopped
- 1 teaspoon chili powder
- 1 teaspoon sweet paprika
- 2 tablespoons avocado oil
- A pinch of salt and black pepper

1.Heat a pan with the oil over medium-high heat, add the scallions and sauté for 5 minutes.

2.Add the rice and the other ingredients except the shrimp, and cook the mix for 15 minutes.

3.Add the shrimp, cook everything for another 5 minutes, divide into bowls and serve.

Nutrition: calories 240, fat 7, fiber 6, carbs 8, protein 14

Lemon Sea Bass

Prep Time: 5 min | **Cook Time:** 12 min | **Serve:** 4

- 4 sea bass fillets, boneless

- 2 tablespoons olive oil

- 3 spring onions, chopped

- 2 tablespoons lemon juice

- Salt and black pepper to the taste

- 2 tablespoons dill, chopped

1.Heat a pan with the oil over medium heat, add the onions and sauté for 2 minutes.

2.Add the fish and the other ingredients, cook everything for 5 minutes on each side, divide the mix between plates.

Nutrition: calories 214, fat 12, fiber 4, carbs 7, protein 17

Trout with Chives Coconut Sauce

Prep Time: 4 min | **Cook Time:** 15 min | **Serve:** 4

- 4 trout fillets, boneless
- 2 spring onions, chopped
- 2 tablespoons olive oil
- 1 cup tomatoes, peeled and crushed
- ¼ cup coconut cream
- 1 tablespoon chives, chopped
- A pinch of salt and black pepper

1.Heat a pan with the oil over medium heat, add the spring onions, tomatoes and the cream and cook for 5 minutes.

2.Add the fish and the rest of the ingredients, toss, cook everything for 10 minutes more, divide between plates.

Nutrition: calories 200, fat 5, fiber 6, carbs 12, protein 12

Salmon and Peppers

Prep Time: 5 min | **Cook Time:** 25 min | **Serve:** 4

- 1 cup roasted red peppers, cut into strips

- 4 salmon fillets, boneless

- ¼ cup chicken stock

- 2 tablespoons olive oil

- 1 yellow onion, chopped

- 1 tablespoon cilantro, chopped

- A pinch of sea salt and black pepper

1.Heat a pan with the oil over medium-high heat, add the onion and sauté for 5 minutes.

2.Add the fish and cook for 5 minutes on each side.

3.Add the rest of the ingredients, introduce the pan in the oven and cook at 390 degrees F for 10 minutes.

4.Divide the mix between plates and serve.

Nutrition: calories 265, fat 7, fiber 5, carbs 15, protein 16

Shrimp and Garlic Beets

Prep Time: 10 min | **Cook Time:** 10 min | **Serve:** 4

- 1 pound shrimp, peeled and deveined

- 2 tablespoons avocado oil

- 2 spring onions, chopped

- 2 garlic cloves, minced

- 1 beet, peeled and cubed

- 1 tablespoon lemon juice

- A pinch of sea salt and black pepper

- 1 teaspoon coconut aminos

1.Heat a pan with the oil over medium-high heat, add the spring onions and the garlic and sauté for 2 minutes.

2.Add the shrimp and the other ingredients, toss, cook the mix for 8 minutes, divide into bowls and serve.

Nutrition: calories 281, fat 6, fiber 7, carbs 11, protein 8

Shrimp and Parsley Corn

Prep Time: 5 min | **Cook Time:** 10 min | **Serve:** 4

- 1 pound shrimp, peeled and deveined
- 2 garlic cloves, minced
- 1 cup corn
- ½ cup veggie stock
- 1 bunch parsley, chopped
- Juice of 1 lime
- 2 tablespoons olive oil
- A pinch of sea salt and black pepper

1.Heat a pan with the oil over medium-high heat, add the garlic and the corn and sauté for 2 minutes.

2.Add the shrimp and the other ingredients, toss, cook everything for 8 minutes more, divide between plates.

Ginger Shrimp Pan

Prep Time: 10 min | **Cook Time:** 10 min | **Serve:** 4

- 1 pound shrimp, peeled and deveined

- 2 tablespoons chili paste

- A pinch of sea salt and black pepper

- 1 tablespoon olive oil

- 1 cup pineapple, peeled and cubed

- ½ teaspoon ginger, grated

- 2 teaspoons almonds, chopped

- 2 tablespoons cilantro, chopped

1

.Heat a pan with the oil over medium-high heat, add the ginger and the chili paste, stir and cook for 2 minutes.

2.Add the shrimp and the other ingredients, toss, cook the mix for 8 minutes more, divide into bowls and serve.

Nutrition: calories 261, fat 4, fiber 7, carbs 15, protein 8

Curry Tilapia

Prep Time: 5 min | **Cook Time:** 20 min | **Serve:** 4

- 1 tablespoon olive oil

- 2 tablespoons green curry paste

- 4 tilapia fillets, boneless

- Juice of ½ lime

- 1 cup canned red kidney beans, drained and rinsed

- 1 tablespoon parsley, chopped

1.Heat a pan with the oil over medium heat, add the fish and cook for 5 minutes on each side.

2.Add the rest of the ingredients, toss gently, cook over medium heat for 10 minutes more, divide between plates.

Nutrition: calories 271, fat 4, fiber 6, carbs 14, protein 7

Oregano Shrimp Pan

Prep Time: 5 min | **Cook Time:** 10 min | **Serve:** 4

- 2 tablespoons olive oil

- 1 pound shrimp, peeled and deveined

- 1 teaspoon rosemary, dried

- 1 teaspoon oregano, dried

- 1 cup corn

- 1 teaspoon smoked paprika

- A pinch of sea salt and black pepper

1.Heat a pan with the oil over medium-high heat, add the shrimp, rosemary and the other ingredients, toss, cook for 10 minutes, divide into bowls and serve.

Nutrition: calories 271, fat 4, fiber 6, carbs 14, protein

15

Cilantro Scallops

Prep Time: 5 min | **Cook Time:** 10 min | **Serve:** 4

- 1 pound sea scallops

- 4 scallions, chopped

- 2 tablespoons olive oil

- 1 tablespoon balsamic vinegar

- 1 tablespoon cilantro, chopped

- A pinch of salt and black pepper

1.Heat a pan with the oil over medium-high heat, add the scallops, the scallions and the other ingredients, toss, cook for 10 minutes, divide into bowls and serve.

Nutrition: calories 300, fat 4, fiber 4, carbs 14, protein 17

Shrimp and Lime Carrots

Prep Time: 5 min | **Cook Time:** 10 min | **Serve:** 4

- 1 pound shrimp, peeled and deveined

- 2 tablespoons olive oil

- ¼ cup vegetable stock

- 2 tablespoons rosemary, chopped

- 2 cups baby carrots, peeled

- 1 tablespoon lime juice

- A pinch of sea salt and black pepper

1.Heat a pan with the oil over medium-high heat, add the carrots, rosemary and the other ingredients except the shrimp, toss and cook for 5 minutes.

2.Add the shrimp, cook the mix for 5 minutes more, divide into bowls and serve.

Nutrition: calories 271, fat 6, fiber 7, carbs 14, protein 18

Cod and Coriander Quinoa

Prep Time: 10 min | **Cook Time:** 25 min | **Serve:** 4

- 3 scallions, chopped

- 2 cups chicken stock

- 1 pound cod fillets, boneless and cubed

- 1 cup black quinoa

- 2 tablespoons olive oil

- 2 celery stalks, chopped

- A pinch of salt and black pepper

- 1 tablespoon coriander, chopped

1.Heat a pan with the oil over medium-high heat, add the scallions and the celery and sauté for 5 minutes.

2.Add the fish and cook for 5 minutes more.

3.Add the rest of the ingredients, toss, cook over medium heat for 15 minutes more, divide everything between plates.

Nutrition: calories 261, fat 4, fiber 6, carbs 14, protein 7

Shrimp and Chives Endives Mix

Prep Time: 5 min | **Cook Time:** 12 min | **Serve:** 4

- 1 pound shrimp, peeled and deveined
- 2 tablespoons avocado oil
- 2 spring onions, chopped
- 2 endives, shredded
- 1 tablespoon balsamic vinegar
- 1 tablespoon chives, minced
- A pinch of sea salt and black pepper

1.Heat a pan with the oil over medium-high heat, add the spring onions, endives and chives, stir and cook for 4 minutes.

2.Add the shrimp and the rest of the ingredients, toss, cook over medium heat for 8 minutes more, divide into bowls.

Nutrition: calories 191, fat 3.3, fiber 8,5 carbs 11.3, protein 29.3

Snapper and Veggies Mix

Prep Time: 5 min | **Cook Time:** 20 min | **Serve:** 4

- 2 tablespoons olive oil
- 2 garlic cloves, minced
- 4 snapper fillets, boneless, skinless and cubed
- 1 tomato, cubed
- 1 zucchini, cubed
- 1 tablespoon coriander, chopped
- ½ teaspoon cumin, ground
- ½ teaspoon rosemary, dried
- A pinch of salt and black pepper

1.Heat a pan with the oil over medium-high heat, add the garlic, tomato and zucchini and cook for 5 minutes.

2.Add the fish and the other ingredients, toss, cook the mix for 15 minutes more, divide it into bowls and serve.

Nutrition: calories 251, fat 4, fiber 6, carbs 14, protein 7

Cinnamon Scallops

Prep Time: 10 min | **Cook Time:** 20 min | **Serve:** 4

- 2 tablespoons olive oil

- 2 jalapenos, chopped

- 1 pound sea scallops

- A pinch of salt and black pepper

- ¼ teaspoon cinnamon powder

- 1 teaspoon garam masala

- 1 teaspoon coriander, ground

- 1 teaspoon cumin, ground

- 2 tablespoons cilantro, chopped

1.Heat a pan with the oil over medium heat, add the jalapenos, cinnamon and the other ingredients except the scallops and cook for 10 minutes.

2.Add the rest of the ingredients, toss, cook for 10 minutes more, divide into bowls and serve.

Nutrition: calories 251, fat 4, fiber 4, carbs 11, protein 17

Tuna with Peppers and Tomatoes

Prep Time: 5 min | **Cook Time:** 20 min | **Serve:** 4

- 1 yellow onion, chopped

- 1 tablespoon olive oil

- 1 pound tuna fillets, boneless, skinless and cubed

- 1 cup tomatoes, chopped

- 1 red pepper, chopped

- 1 teaspoon sweet paprika

- 1 tablespoon coriander, chopped

1.Heat a pan with the oil over medium heat, add the onions and the pepper and cook for 5 minutes.

2.Add the fish and the other ingredients, cook everything for 15 minutes, divide between plates and serve.

Nutrition: calories 215, fat 4, fiber 7, carbs 14, protein 7

Tuna with Tomatoes and Kale

Prep Time: 5 min | **Cook Time:** 20 min | **Serve:** 4

- 1 pound tuna fillets, boneless, skinless and cubed
- A pinch of salt and black pepper
- 2 tablespoons olive oil
- 1 cup kale, torn
- ½ cup cherry tomatoes, cubed
- 1 yellow onion, chopped

1.Heat a pan with the oil over medium heat, add the onion and sauté for 5 minutes.

2.Add the tuna and the other ingredients, toss, cook everything for 15 minutes more, divide between plates.

Nutrition: calories 251, fat 4, fiber 7, carbs 14, protein 7

Lemongrass Mackerel

Prep Time: 10 min | **Cook Time:** 25 min | **Serve:** 4

- 4 mackerel fillets, skinless and boneless
- 2 tablespoons olive oil
- 1 tablespoon ginger, grated
- 2 lemongrass sticks, chopped
- 2 red chilies, chopped
- Juice of 1 lime
- A handful parsley, chopped

1.In a roasting pan, combine the mackerel with the oil, ginger and the other ingredients, toss and bake at 390 degrees F for 25 minutes.

2.Divide everything between plates and serve.

Nutrition: calories 251, fat 3, fiber 4, carbs 14, protein 8

Almond Scallops Mix

Prep Time: 5 min | **Cook Time:** 10 min | **Serve:** 4

- 1 pound scallops

- 2 tablespoons olive oil

- 4 scallions, chopped

- A pinch of salt and black pepper

- ½ cup mushrooms, sliced

- 2 tablespoon almonds, chopped

- 1 cup coconut cream

1.Heat a pan with the oil over medium heat, add the scallions and the mushrooms and sauté for 2 minutes.

2.Add the scallops and the other ingredients, toss, cook over medium heat for 8 minutes more, divide into bowls and serve.

Nutrition: calories 322, fat 23.7, fiber 2.2, carbs 8.1, protein 21.6

Scallops and Rosemary Potatoes

Prep Time: 5 min | **Cook Time:** 22 min | **Serve:** 4

- 1 pound scallops
- ½ teaspoon rosemary, dried
- ½ teaspoon oregano, dried
- 2 tablespoons avocado oil
- 1 yellow onion, chopped
- 2 sweet potatoes, peeled and cubed
- ½ cup chicken stock
- 1 tablespoon cilantro, chopped
- A pinch of salt and black pepper

1.Heat a pan with the oil over medium heat, add the onion and sauté for 2 minutes.

2.Add the sweet potatoes and the stock, toss and cook for 10 minutes more.

3.Add the scallops and the remaining ingredients, toss, cook for another 10 minutes, divide everything into bowls.

Nutrition: calories 211, fat 2, fiber 4.1, carbs 26.9, protein 20.7

Salmon with Shrimp and Arugula Bowls

Prep Time: 5 min | **Cook Time:** 0 min | **Serve:** 4

- 1 cup smoked salmon, boneless and flaked

- 1 cup shrimp, peeled, deveined and cooked ½ cup baby arugula

- 1 tablespoon lemon juice

- 2 spring onions, chopped

- 1 tablespoon olive oil

- A pinch of sea salt and black pepper

1.In a salad bowl, combine the salmon with the shrimp and the other ingredients, toss and serve.

Nutrition: calories 210, fat 6, fiber 5, carbs 10, protein 12

Shrimp, Walnuts and Dates Salad

Prep Time: 10 min | **Cook Time:** 0 min | **Serve:** 4

- 1 pound shrimp, cooked, peeled and deveined
- 2 cups baby spinach
- 2 tablespoons walnuts, chopped
- 1 cup cherry tomatoes, halved
- 1 tablespoon lemon juice
- ½ cup dates, chopped
- 2 tablespoons avocado oil

1.In a salad bowl, mix the shrimp with the spinach, walnuts and the other ingredients, toss and serve.

Nutrition: calories 243, fat 5.4, fiber 3.3, carbs 21.6, protein 28.3

Salmon and Cucumber Salad

Prep Time: 10 min | **Cook Time:** 0 min | **Serve:** 4

- 1 pound smoked salmon, boneless, skinless and flaked
- 2 spring onions, chopped
- 2 tablespoons avocado oil
- ½ cup baby arugula
- 1 cup watercress
- 1 tablespoon lemon juice
- 1 cucumber, sliced
- 1 avocado, peeled, pitted and roughly cubed A pinch of sea salt and black pepper

1.In a salad bowl, mix the salmon with the spring onions, watercress and the other ingredients, toss and serve.

Nutrition: calories 261, fat 15.8, fiber 4.4, carbs 8.2, protein 22.7

Indian Shrimp with Coriander and Turmeric

Prep Time: 5 min | **Cook Time:** 1 hour | **Serve:** 2

- 4 scallions, chopped
- 1 tablespoon olive oil
- 1 pound shrimp, peeled and deveined
- ½ teaspoon garam masala
- ½ teaspoon coriander, ground
- ½ teaspoon turmeric powder
- 1 tablespoon lime juice
- ½ cup chicken stock
- ¼ cup lime leaves, torn

1.In your slow cooker, mix the shrimp with the oil, scallions, masala, and the other ingredients, toss, put the lid on and cook on High for 1 hour.

2.Divide the mix into bowls and serve.

Nutrition: 344 calories,52.4g protein, 6.2g carbohydrates, 11.1g fat, 0.9g fiber, 478mg cholesterol, 750mg sodium, 485mg potassium.

Shrimp and Kale Garnish

Prep Time: 5 min | **Cook Time:** 1 hour | **Serve:** 2

- 1 pound shrimp, peeled and deveined
- ½ cup cherry tomatoes halved
- 1 cup baby kale
- ½ cup chicken stock
- 1 tablespoon olive oil
- Juice of 1 lime
- ½ teaspoon sweet paprika
- 1 tablespoon cilantro, chopped

1.In your slow cooker, mix the shrimp with the cherry tomatoes, kale, and the other ingredients, toss, put the lid on and cook on High for 1 hour.

2.Divide the mix into bowls and serve.

Nutrition: 360 calories,53.7g protein, 9.2g carbohydrates, 11.4g fat, 1.5g fiber, 478mg cholesterol, 768mg sodium, 403mg potassium.

Trout Bowls with Olives

Prep Time: 5 min | **Cook Time:** 3 hours | **Serve:** 4

- 1 pound trout fillets, boneless, skinless, and cubed
- 1 cup kalamata olives, pitted and chopped
- 1 cup baby spinach
- 2 garlic cloves, minced
- 1 tablespoon olive oil
- Juice of ½ lime
- 1 tablespoon parsley, chopped

1.In your slow cooker, mix the trout with the olives, spinach, and the other ingredients, toss, put the lid on and cook on Low for 3 hours.

2.Divide everything into bowls and serve.

Nutrition: 288 calories,30.8g protein, 2.9g carbohydrates, 16.7g fat, 1.3g fiber, 84mg cholesterol, 376mg sodium, 581mg potassium.

Calamari Curry with Coriander

Prep Time: 10 min | **Cook Time:** 3 hours | **Serve:** 4

- 1 pound calamari rings
- ½ tablespoon yellow curry paste
- 1 cup of coconut milk
- ½ teaspoon turmeric powder
- ½ cup chicken stock
- 2 garlic cloves, minced
- ½ tablespoon coriander, chopped
- 2 tablespoons lemon juice

1.In your slow cooker, mix the rings with the curry paste, coconut milk, and the other ingredients, toss, put the lid on and cook on High for 3 hours.

2.Divide the curry into bowls and serve.

Nutrition: 213 calories,3.6g protein, 9.1g carbohydrates, 19.1g fat, 1.8g fiber, 0mg cholesterol, 157mg sodium, 183mg potassium.

Balsamic Trout with Cumin

Prep Time: 10 min | **Cook Time:** 3 hours | **Serve:** 4

- 1 pound trout fillets, boneless

- ½ cup chicken stock

- 2 garlic cloves, minced

- 2 tablespoons balsamic vinegar

- ½ teaspoon cumin, ground

- 1 tablespoon parsley, chopped

- 1 tablespoon olive oil

1.In your slow cooker, mix the trout with the stock, garlic, and the other ingredients, toss gently, put the lid on and cook on High for 3 hours.

2.Divide the mix between plates and serve.

Nutrition: 252 calories,30.5g protein, 0.8g carbohydrates, 13.3g fat, 0.1g fiber, 84mg cholesterol, 173mg sodium, 548mg potassium.

Oregano Shrimp Bowls with Garlic

Prep Time: 10 min | **Cook Time:** 1 hour | **Serve:** 4

- 1 pound shrimp, peeled and deveined
- ½ cup cherry tomatoes halved
- ½ cup baby spinach
- 1 tablespoon lime juice
- 1 tablespoon oregano, chopped
- ¼ cup fish stock
- ½ teaspoon sweet paprika
- 2 garlic cloves, chopped

1.In your slow cooker, mix the shrimp with the cherry tomatoes, spinach, and the other ingredients, toss, put the lid on and cook on High for 1 hour.

2.Divide everything between plates and serve.

Nutrition: 161 calories,27.3g protein, 6.8g carbohydrates, 2.2g fat, 1.5g fiber, 239mg cholesterol, 312mg sodium, 413mg potassium.

Sweet Salmon Mix

Prep Time: 10 min | **Cook Time:** 2 hours | **Serve:** 4

- 1 pound salmon fillets, boneless
- 1 cup strawberries, halved
- ½ cup of orange juice
- Zest of 1 lemon, grated
- 4 scallions, chopped
- 1 teaspoon balsamic vinegar
- 1 tablespoon chives, chopped

1.In your slow cooker, mix the salmon with the strawberries, orange juice, and the other ingredients, toss, put the lid on and cook on High for 2 hours.

2.Divide everything into bowls and serve.

Nutrition: 181 calories,22.7g protein, 7.1g carbohydrates, 7.2g fat, 1.2g fiber, 50mg cholesterol, 53mg sodium, 597mg potassium.

Shrimps and Salmon Mix

Prep Time: 5 m | **Cook Time:** 1 h and 30 m| **Serve:** 4

- 1 pound shrimp, peeled and deveined
- ½ pound salmon fillets, boneless and cubed 1 cup cherry tomatoes, halved ½ cup chicken stock
- ½ teaspoon chili powder
- ½ teaspoon rosemary, dried
- 1 tablespoon parsley, chopped
- 2 tablespoons tomato sauce
- 2 garlic cloves, minced

1.In your slow cooker, combine the shrimp with the salmon, tomatoes, and the other ingredients, toss gently, put the lid on, and cook on High for 1 hour and 30 minutes.

2.Divide the mix into bowls and serve.

Nutrition: 225 calories,37.6g protein, 4.8g carbohydrates, 5.7g fat, 0.9g fiber, 264mg cholesterol, 444mg sodium, 563mg potassium.

Shrimp and Cilantro Bowls

Prep Time: 5 min | **Cook Time:** 2 hours | **Serve:** 2

- 1-pound shrimp, peeled and deveined
- ½ cup chicken stock
- 1 cup cauliflower florets
- ½ teaspoon turmeric powder
- ½ teaspoon coriander, ground
- ½ cup tomato passata
- 1 tablespoon cilantro, chopped

1.In your slow cooker, mix the cauliflower with the stock, turmeric, and the other ingredients except for the shrimp, toss, put the lid on and cook on High for 1 hour.

2.Add the shrimp, toss, cook on High for 1 more hour, divide into bowls and serve.

Nutrition: 294 calories,53.2g protein, 8.2g carbohydrates, 4.1g fat, 1.4g fiber, 478mg cholesterol, 760mg sodium, 554mg potassium.

Lightning Source UK Ltd.
Milton Keynes UK
UKHW020634190421
382237UK00001B/35

9 781801 456241